Jackie Robinson

by Lola M. Schaefer

Consulting Editor: Gail Saunders-Smith, Ph.D.

Consultant: James L. Gates Jr., Library Director,
National Baseball Hall of Fame and Museum, Inc.
Cooperstown, New York

Pebble Books are published by Capstone Press
151 Good Counsel Drive, P.O. Box 669, Mankato, Minnesota 56002
http://www.capstone-press.com

1 2 3 4 5 6 07 06 05 04 03 02

Library of Congress Cataloging-in-Publication Data
Schaefer, Lola M., 1950–
  Jackie Robinson / by Lola M. Schaefer.
    p. cm.—(First biographies)
  Summary: A brief biography of the man who was the first African American
baseball player on a major league team, as well as the first African American elected
to the Baseball Hall of Fame.
  Includes bibliographical references and index.
  ISBN 0-7368-1435-3 (hardcover)
  ISBN 0-7368-9412-8 (paperback)
  1. Robinson, Jackie, 1919–1972—Juvenile literature. 2. Baseball players—United
States—Biography—Juvenile literature. 3. African American baseball players—
Biography—Juvenile literature. [1. Robinson, Jackie, 1919-1972. 2. Baseball players.
3. African Americans—Biography.] I. Title. II. First biographies (Mankato, Minn.)
GV865.R6 S29 2003
796.357'092—dc21   2002001217

Note to Parents and Teachers

The First Biographies series supports national history standards for
units on people and culture. This book describes and illustrates the
life of Jackie Robinson. The images support early readers in
understanding the text. This book also introduces early readers to
subject-specific vocabulary words, which are defined in the Words
to Know section. Early readers may need assistance to read some
words and to use the Table of Contents, Words to Know, Read
More, Internet Sites, and Index/Word List sections of the book.

Table of Contents

Young Jackie. 5

A Life in Sports 11

Major League Baseball. 17

Words to Know 22

Read More 23

Internet Sites. 23

Index/Word List. 24

Time Line

1919
born

4

Jackie Robinson was born in Georgia in 1919. His family was poor. They moved to California to make a better life.

Jackie at about three years old

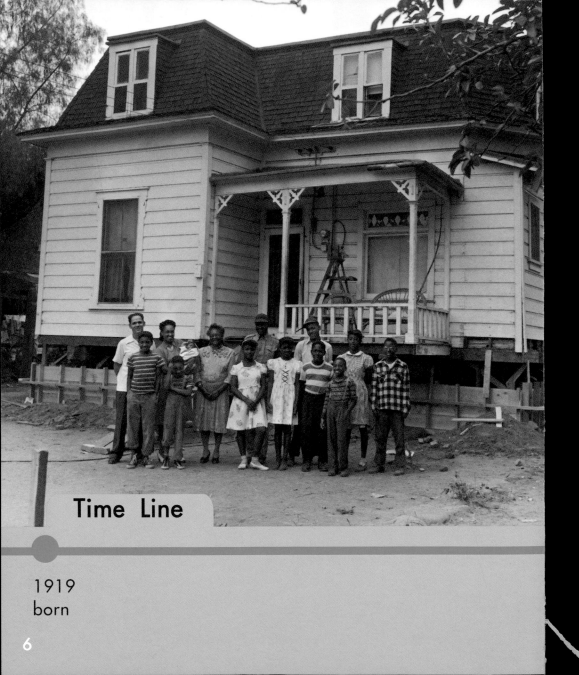

Time Line

Jackie went to school. He worked hard at many jobs. He gave the money he earned to his mother. She bought food and clothes for the family.

 Jackie and his family in California

Time Line

1919
born

8

Some white people did not like African Americans. These people treated Jackie and his family unfairly. But Jackie was proud of himself and his family.

◀ Jackie (second from left) and his family

Time Line

1919
born

Jackie was a sports star in high school and college. He won many awards. He left college to earn more money for his family.

Jackie jumping in a college track meet

Time Line

1919
born

1942
joins the
U.S. Army

Jackie joined the U.S. Army in 1942. He worked hard to be a good soldier. But some Army officers treated him unfairly because he was an African American.

Jackie in his Army uniform

Time Line

1919
born

1942
joins the
U.S. Army

1945
plays for Kansas
City Monarchs

In 1945, Jackie played baseball for the Kansas City Monarchs. This team was in the Negro American League. At that time, African Americans could not play on major league teams.

Time Line

1919
born

1942
joins the
U.S. Army

1945
plays for Kansas
City Monarchs

1946
plays for
Montreal Royals

16

In 1946, Jackie played for the Montreal Royals. In 1947, he became the first African American player on a major league team. That team was the Brooklyn Dodgers.

1947
plays for
Brooklyn Dodgers

Time Line

| 1919 born | 1942 joins the U.S. Army | 1945 plays for Kansas City Monarchs | 1946 plays for Montreal Royals |

Jackie played for the Brooklyn Dodgers for 10 years. He was a great player. But some people still treated him unfairly because he was an African American.

Jackie's teammates congratulating him after he hit a home run in a 1951 playoff game

1947–1956
plays for
Brooklyn Dodgers

Time Line

1919
born

1942
joins the
U.S. Army

1945
plays for Kansas
City Monarchs

1946
plays for
Montreal Royals

Jackie was elected to the National Baseball Hall of Fame in 1962. He was the first African American honored there. Jackie Robinson died in 1972.

Jackie holding his National Baseball Hall of Fame award

1947–1956
plays for
Brooklyn Dodgers

1962
is elected to National
Baseball Hall of Fame

1972
dies

Words to Know

African American—a citizen of the United States with an African background

award—an honor or prize

college—a school people attend after high school

earn—to receive payment for working

elect—to choose someone

hall of fame—a place where important people are honored

honor—to give praise to someone

major league—the highest playing level of professional baseball

officer—a person who gives orders to other people in the armed forces

proud—feeling pleased and happy about oneself

soldier—someone who fights in the military

unfairly—not fair or not right

Read More

Abraham, Philip. *Jackie Robinson.* Real People. New York: Children's Press, 2002.

De Marco, Tony. *Jackie Robinson.* Chanhassen, Minn.: Child's World, 2002.

Raatma, Lucia. *Jackie Robinson.* Early Biographies. Minneapolis: Compass Point Books, 2001.

Internet Sites

Breaking the Barriers
http://www.chron.com/content/chronicle/
sports/special/barriers

Jackie Robinson
http://www.sikids.com/news/blackhistory/jackierobinson.html

Jackie Robinson Photos
http://www.sportingnews.com/features/
jackie/photos.html

National Baseball Hall of Fame: Jackie Robinson
http://www.baseballhalloffame.org/
hofers_and_honorees/hofer_bios/robinson_jackie.htm

Index/Word List

awards, 11
baseball, 15, 21
born, 5
Brooklyn Dodgers,
    17, 19
California, 5
college, 11
died, 21
family, 5, 7, 9, 11
Georgia, 5
jobs, 7
Kansas City
    Monarchs, 15
major league, 15, 17

money, 7, 11
Montreal Royals, 17
mother, 7
moved, 5
National Baseball Hall
    of Fame, 21
Negro American
    League, 15
poor, 5
proud, 9
school, 7, 11
soldier, 13
sports, 11
U.S. Army, 13

Word Count: 235
Early-Intervention Level: 22

Editorial Credits
Martha E. H. Rustad, editor; Heather Kindseth, series designer; Linda Clavel,
    illustrator; Patrick D. Dentinger, book designer; Wanda Winch, photo researcher;
    Karen Risch, product planning editor

Photo Credits
Corbis/Bettman, 10, 18, 20
Hulton/Archive by Getty Images, cover, 1, 4, 6, 8, 16; Sporting News, 14
National Baseball Hall of Fame Library, Cooperstown, NY, 12

12/02